Nelson the Noun

Written by Coert Voorhees
Illustrations by Powerhouse Animation

Meet the Parts of Speech

I name a specific person, place, thing, or idea. It's a big responsibility, naming things—a responsibility that requires a certain attention to detail.

Vinny the Action Verb

Some people say I'm all over the place. Some people call me a ball of energy. I take that as a compliment, because I just like to go, go, go!

I take the place of one or more Nouns or Pronouns. I always want the Noun's job, and I hang out with the Verb and Adjective.

I'm perfectly happy to link Nouns and Pronouns with the appropriate Adjectives, but it's not like I'm going to expend a lot of energy doing so.

I modify a Noun or Pronoun. I tell what kind, which one, how many, or how much. I pride myself on being the most artistic of the parts of speech.

Gather 'round everybody and let's have ourselves a wonderful time. I just love bringing words and groups of words together, don't you?

I modify a Verb, Adjective, or other Adverb. I tell how, when, where, to what extent, and under what condition. I often end in –ly, but I don't have to.

Izzy the Interjection

I express emotion!! Yep, I'm always here, always ready with my commas and exclamation points, just in case.

They call me Preposition because I'm pre-positioned. I'm first. At the front. Before every other word in the phrase? Got it?

I am a chameleon. A spy. An undercover operative. I infiltrate the sentence and act as whatever part of speech suits me.

NELSON THE NOUN

Graphic Design by Mckee Frazior
Printed by Friesens, Altona, Manitoba, Canada

This book is typeset in Komika Text

Distributed throughout the world by Ingram Publisher Services
www.ingrambook.com

Printed in Canada

Before Nelson opened up his own place, he worked at the Noun Office.

His job was to name people, places, things, and ideas.

He worked hard because he knew that Roger the pronoun always wanted to take his place.

Organization was extremely important to Nelson.

Concrete Noun Day was his favorite. He loved naming what he could observe with his five senses.
computer
vase
lederhosen

Collective Noun Day was when Nelson used a singular noun to name a group. It was his least favorite day by far.
smack of jellyfish
cloud of mosquitoes
herd of elephants

Nelson was overwhelmed.
He needed a break.
I'm getting out of here.
Roger, take over.
Really?

He packed light, only taking some of his favorite abstract nouns with him.

He said his goodbyes.
Don't go.
We need you.
Roger can handle this.

I'll miss you most of all, platypus.
Then Nelson the noun left Grammaropolis.

Nelson arrived at a desert island. He quickly named some of the nouns he saw, just to get it over with.

After that, he settled in for a well-earned rest.

At first, Nelson loved his time away.
PEACE
CONTENTMENT

Run!
Dance!
After a while, however, he started to miss his friends.
Without Vinny the action verb, he couldn't do anything.

He missed the other nouns and pronouns, and he missed Connie the conjunction, too.

Without Jake the adjective, he couldn't describe the sunset.
awesome
gorgeous

He tried to console himself with the abstract nouns he'd packed, but "courage" and "happiness" were nowhere to be found.

He didn't even have Izzy the interjection to help him express his dismay.
Alas!
Oh, no.
Leaving Grammaropolis had been a terrible idea, so Nelson packed up and headed for home.

Person
Place
Thing
HER
HIM
THEM
THERE
WHEREVER
HERE
THOSE
THIS
WHOEVER
IT
THESE

He discovered that things had not gone well without him.

Nelson got right to work. He started with the compound nouns: words stuck together to make a single noun.
Compound Nouns
eggplant
windshield
jack-in-the-box
toothpaste
grasshopper
seafood

Nelson had the office back to normal in no time.

Common Noun
Proper Noun
Cleveland
city
You look happy.
document
When in the course
Declaration of Independence
aybe I just needed some time off.
neighbor
Reginald
We could use a little help out here!

NOUN OFFICE
You've got to be kidding me.
Statue Of Li
What's this called?
Dude.

Nelson's
Noun Notes

PERSON

Ava is the most thoughtful girl in our entire school.

PLACE

Zak ate his lunch at a park in Chicago.

THING

There is a small stack of pennies on my dresser.

IDEA

We should all fight for fairness and equality.

A noun names a person, place, thing, or idea.

COMMON NOUNS

A **common noun** names a general person, place, thing, or idea.

EXAMPLES

restaurant
lady
volcanoes

PROPER NOUNS

A proper noun names a specific person, place, thing, or idea.

CONCRETE NOUNS

A **concrete noun** names a person, place, or thing that can be perceived by one or more of the five senses.

The **receptionist** yelled at me when I brought my **platypus** into the **museum**.

EXAMPLES

receptionist
platypus
museum

ABSTRACT NOUNS

An **abstract noun** is an idea or quality that can not be perceived by any of the five senses.

EXAMPLES

honor
courage

COMPOUND NOUNS

An compound noun is two or more words combined to make a single noun that names a person, place, thing, or idea. It can be one single word, two words, or words connected by hyphens.

EXAMPLES

One word: shortcake
Two words: swimming pool
Hyphenated: mother-in-law

COLLECTIVE NOUNS

An **collective noun** is a singular noun that names a group.

EXAMPLES

school of fish
armory of aardvarks
squad of police

CPSIA information can be obtained
at www.ICGtesting.com
Printed in the USA
BVHW020504110519
547997BV00002B/6/P

9 781644 420157